The Terrace Times
COOK BOOK

PERTH FREMANTLE
EDITION

Illustrations
by Tish Phillips

Concept Text and Design
by Helen Arbib

ALSO PUBLISHED BY THE TERRACE TIMES

Minimum Effort Maximum Effect
Cook Books . . .
  Paddington Edition
  The Rocks Edition
  Balmain Edition
  Looking at Cooking
  Melbourne Edition
  City of Sydney Edition
  Brisbane Edition
Minimum Effort Maximum Effect
Garden Book . . .
  The Tiny Utopia

PUBLISHED BY WILLIAM COLLINS, U.K.

Minimum Effort Maximum Effect
Cook Book . . .
  London Edition

DEDICATED TO ALL MY TEST EATERS
WITHOUT WHOM ALL MY TEST COOKING
WOULD NOT JUST BE USELESS BUT NO FUN AT ALL

My special thanks to Ansett Airlines of Australia
who not only helped make this book possible,
but who also made the flights between Perth and
Sydney a thoroughly enjoyable experience instead of an exhausting necessity.

$5.95 Volume Nine
Recommended Retail Price

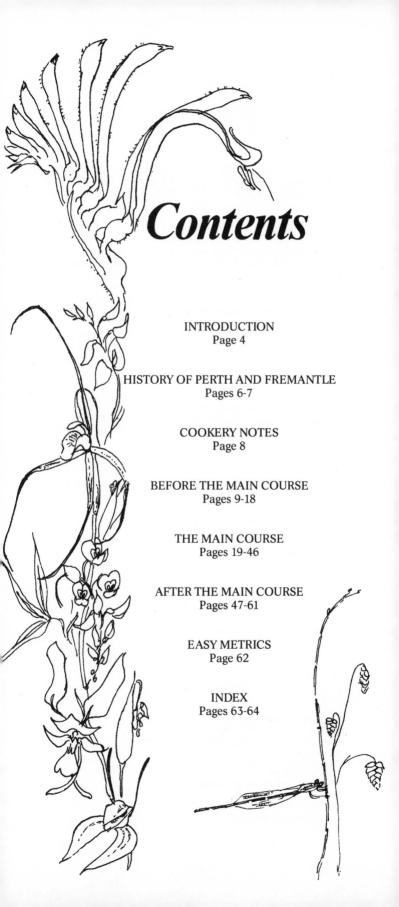

Contents

Introduction

It has been very exciting to be able to visit Western Australia at last, to research for this PERTH FREMANTLE Minimum Effort Maximum Effect COOK BOOK. The ninth in the series.

Writing and publishing a series of cook books — any books — could easily become monotonous and boring. But I find each one a new adventure and a new challenge. It doesn't get easier! But it's a wonderful excuse to experiment with new dishes, their countries of origin as varied as those of Australians themselves. A marvellous incentive to explore Australia's early days, which I used to take for granted. And a very happy way to make new friends.

But that's my side of the story. Now I have to wait and hope that Perth and Fremantle will like their book. What I don't doubt is that everyone else will find their history as fascinating as I have done.

The illustrator for a book like this has to be a special kind of person, and is not always easy to find. So we are very lucky to have well-known West Australian artist and designer Tish Phillips, who really enjoyed this opportunity to draw the historic buildings and wild flowers she loves.

It is always sad to come to the end of a book, with so much left unsaid and undrawn. But at least it gives us a reason to think, some day, about another one.

Helen Arbib

THE TERRACE TIMES
15 ROSLYNDALE AVENUE WOOLLAHRA
NSW 2025 AUSTRALIA

First published 1982
Concept and text ©by Helen Arbib 1982
Illustrations ©by Tish Phillips 1982
National Library of Australia card number and
ISBN 0 9598486 8 1
Wholly designed and set up in Australia
Typesetting by The Word Mill
and Hartland & Hyde Phototypesetting
Printed in Hong Kong through Bookbuilders Ltd

THE ROUND HOUSE, Arthur's Head, Fremantle
is the oldest building in the State, with an unusual twelve-sided outer wall. It stands near the edge of a precipice overlooking the harbour; a sad place, built in 1831 as a gaol for 'minor offenders', who were placed in stocks in the courtyard or locked up in one of the twelve small cells surrounding it. Whales entered the harbour regularly then and whaling was a major local industry; even the lamps were lit with "odiferous" whale oil. The tunnel under the gaol was dug in 1837 to allow the Fremantle Whaling Company easy access between jetty and High Street.

History of Perth

Although West Australia's unique wild flowers, some of which decorate the pages which divide our recipes, bloom for only a brief six weeks in the Spring, they have become the State's biggest tourist attraction. But there was little thought for flowers in the first tough years of settlement.

The existence of Western Australia was widely known for many hundreds of years. Great numbers of Dutch ships engaged in the East India trade approached the coast in the 17th and 18th centuries, and historic relics from some of the shipwrecks at that time have been painstakingly restored and displayed in Fremantle. British and French navigators were luckier, because of all the work done by the Dutch to chart the coastline, and also because of advances in navigation, and French influence is reflected by some of the remaining place names along the coast.

But we are talking about the history of Perth and Fremantle, which began with British occupation in 1829, following an enthusiastic survey by Captain James Stirling in 1827. Captain Charles Howe Fremantle of *H.M.S. Challenger*, a 603 ton 28 gun frigate, was despatched by a government nervous of French colonial aspirations, to "that part of 'New Holland' not included within the territory of New South Wales," and four months later raised the Union Jack at the seaport to be named in his honour. That was on May 2. On June 18, Captain Stirling, who had returned as Governor on board the transport *Parmelia*, formally proclaimed the Swan River Settlement ... which would become the Colony and then the State of Western Australia. And on August 12, an official party rowed up the river to christen Perth as its capital.

The Parmelia carried 69 passengers: the Governor, his family and staff of eight, together with mechanics and artisans and their families and servants. It also carried 33 horses, 51 heads of cattle, 200 sheep, trees, plants and seeds. Further boatloads over the next year or so increased the population to almost 2,000 people said to be "far superior, from a social and moral point of view, to those of any other Australian Colony, or perhaps any other Colony in the world. Gentlemen of culture and good position, nephews of noblemen, and sons of men of high social standing." And, presumably, women to match. But they had come expecting a "land of promise," and many of them were unwilling or unable to face the hardships and privations that awaited them.

Those who stayed must have been incredibly resilient. At first, even women and children had to sleep on the beaches, with only umbrellas to protect them from the rain and driving winds that swept up from the Indian Ocean. Champagne cases and pianos had to be broken up to provide makeshift shelter, trenches dug to keep away wild animals and snakes. The sandy soil proved hard to cultivate, stock died from eating poisonous plants or got lost in the bush, there was little money around and, at one time, salt beef condemned and buried was dug up and sold for a shilling a pound.

and Fremantle

But life went on. Somehow it always does. Balls were held in a tent in Government House grounds that overlooked the river. The only means of transport between Fremantle and Perth was by boat and the Governor visited Fremantle and the Swan River district in his official galley, a single-decked vessel with sails and oars, painted white with a red and white awning and manned by four sailors in white regulation dress in summer, blue in winter. "Officers and gentlemen" entered the river from bathing machines, so as not to be stared at by the "lower orders." While they, in their turn, took their pleasures by staying up late to sing and drink. And the Aborigines, in theirs, camped in hundreds at the Third Swamp (later to become Perth's Hyde Park), waiting for their corroborees to begin, and peeling the tremendous paper bark trees that grew there, to make their huts.

Progress was slow, because so many people came and went. There were the regulations issued by the Colonial Office in London that provided for land to be granted according to the capital brought in by each individual, at 1s.6d an acre. The result was that more than a million acres was handed out in two to three years and later settlers, "industrious and persevering men," important for the development of a new colony, found the best land taken up by speculators, and moved on. Then, when the British government revoked the scheme and decreed that land should be sold for not less than 5s. an acre, many colonists packed their bags in fury and sailed for Van Diemen's Land (Tasmania).

The events that shaped Fremantle and Perth are often divided into three main periods.

1829-50, the pioneering period, covers the struggle to survive far from home in a new environment, and the first steps taken to establish the colony in spite of the odds against it. In 1833 alone, a legislative council was appointed, a civil court established, and the first newspaper published.

1850-1885 was the period dominated by the importation of British finance, and the transportation of British convicts — which ended in 1868. It was originally determined that no prisoners of any kind would be brought into the colony, but shortage of labour proved as serious a handicap to development as shortage of money, and we owe many of the finest old buildings in Fremantle and Perth to those convict years.

1886-1979, the final period, saw the boom years that resulted from the discovery of gold (at one stage, the output was valued at £7 million a year) and the transformation of Fremantle into a major trading port, of Perth into a major city. Federation in 1901. War in 1914-18. More boom years, the depression — when almost one man in four had no job, recovery, war again, reconstruction and another boom, with huge fortunes made and Perth suburbs doubling in number.

It's AMAZING, all that can happen in just 150 years.

7

Cookery Notes

Eating has never been just a matter of survival. In every kind of society, however simple or sophisticated, it is the most generally accepted way to initiate and maintain human relationships. Even the English word for *companion* comes from Latin and French words that mean "one who eats bread with another."

Which is probably why I feel so strongly about minimum effort maximum effect cooking: producing delicious food for people we care about is an integral part of that caring. But to wear ourselves out producing it, and then have no energy left to enjoy sharing it, is pretty stupid.

So let's relax and enjoy ourselves in the kitchen, and remember: —

*To take note that, while appetites and menus vary, all the recipes in this book are loosely planned for 6-8 people. And that they allow for the fact that can sizes also vary; nothing terrible will happen if a little less or a little more of any canned ingredient is added.

*To have, in all our menus, at least some streamlined recipes that are as easy to read as they are to cook.

*To include dishes that can be prepared a day or several hours ahead when possible, and reduce the stress of trying to get everything done at once. *Such recipes are marked — for the first time — with an A. before the cooking instructions.* A good idea?

*To process back-up foods when there is time: breadcrumbs, grated orange and lemon rind and juice, chopped herbs, boiled rice, etc. Have them ready-frozen for when time is short.

*To cook in flameproof oven-to-tableware (it's worth every penny) and avoid unnecessary handling.

*To use metric cups and spoons, as specified (all measures are level) and save weighing-time.

*To preheat the oven 10°C higher than needed; reset it correctly when food, and cold air, go in.

*Not to be intimidated. To accept that, while homemade stock, freshly grown herbs (freshly grown anything) and freshly ground pepper obviously produce the best results, we can still create beautiful food without them.

*Most important of all, not to panic when something goes wrong. I often find a disaster is the best part of a party, with everyone having a great time trying to work out how they would solve the problem!

H.A.

Before the Main Course

"The jetty at Perth during the summer season is a very inconvenient landing place . . . The present practice of landing passengers pickapack, the boatmen being obliged to wade through mud for the extent of thirty or forty yards, is hazardous and unpleasant, and one most persons we should imagine would readily pay a trifling sum to be removed from. We strongly recommend either the extension of the old jetty, or the formation of a new one."
THE PERTH GAZETTE, February 1833.

Appetisers

It's tempting, when we are busy, to serve drinks with something from a packet or jar, and devote our time and energy to the food to follow. Yet a delicious appetiser is far more likely to set the scene for a delicious meal. And it can be fun to make.

Prawn Savoury Mousse is one easy example.

Soften
    2 teaspoons gelatine, in
    ½ cup unsweetened tomato juice
Set aside. Bring to boil in large saucepan
    1 cup unsweetened tomato juice
Remove from heat and stir in softened gelatine until dissolved. Blend in with whisk
    300g carton sour cream
When completely blended, stir in
    1 tablespoon lemon juice
    2 tablespoons soy sauce and ½ teaspoon salt
    3 tablespoons finely chopped chives
Add and mix through evenly
    1 200g can tiny picnic prawns, well drained
Pour mixture into 5-6 cup terrine or similar dish. Cover. Chill at least 3 hours, roughing up surface with fork before fully set.

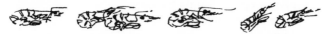

Little Stuffed Mushrooms can be prepared early in the day, heated before serving.

Allowing 2 each, finely chop stalks from
    12-16 small flat mushrooms
Mix together thoroughly with
    1 tablespoon finely chopped anchovy fillets
    100g fresh white breadcrumbs
    2 tablespoons finely chopped parsley
    1½ tablespoons finely chopped chives
    3 teaspoons lemon juice
    ¼ teaspoon black pepper
Pack mixture into mushroom caps. Top with
    100-125g grated Cheddar cheese
Set aside. When required, cook on greased oven tray in 200C oven 15 minutes or until cheese has melted and browned slightly.
*Larger quantities make an excellent entrée.

"The Savoy Hotel is the leading Hotel in Western Australia, Containing 80 Luxurious Rooms, each opening to the outer air. Tariff 12s6d per day, £4.4s per week."
THE AUSTRALIAN HOUSEHOLD GUIDE, Perth 1916.

Guacamole is a speedy dip. In Mexico, it is also served as a salad.

Remove and reserve stones from
    2 large ripe avocados
Scoop out flesh and mash it lightly.
Blend in immediately, to prevent browning
    2 tablespoons lime or lemon juice
    ½ teaspoon salt
As recipes vary greatly, add any or all of the following, tasting as you go
    2 tablespoons finely chopped onion
    1 clove garlic, crushed
    2 teaspoons chopped coriander
    ⅛ teaspoon cayenne pepper
For smoother consistency, blend in
    1 tablespoon olive oil or egg mayonnaise
Add stones — they also prevent discolouring.
Cover and chill. Serve (stoneless) with
    Mexican corn chips
*For salad, add to other ingredients
    1 tomato, peeled and finely chopped.

Cheese Morsels. The French would call them *amuse guele*, a tasty little something to "amuse your mouth".

A. Allow to thaw slightly 2 sheets
    frozen ready rolled puff pastry
Cut into 8 sticks
    250g packet tasty mature cheese 3cm-thick
Halve sticks to make 16 cheese pieces.
Cut each pastry sheet into 4 equal panels.
Brush them very lightly with water.
Position 2 cheese pieces on each panel so as to fold pastry easily over them. Press edges to seal and cut away surplus pastry, to make 16 little packets ... if made ahead, refrigerate or freeze in plastic bag, but return to room temperature before cooking.
When required, deep-fry 3-4 at a time, just until puffy and golden, in oil heated until test piece of pastry sizzles. Drain on paper towelling and serve hot.

Melba Toast, to serve with soup, is a great way to use up leftover bread.

Cut into thinnest possible slices
    stale white bread
Remove crusts and bake on biscuit sheet in 125C oven until golden and crisp and curling at edges. Store in sealed container.

Soups

A friend of mine, and her family, spend countless hours boiling up huge pots of beef, bones, and vegetables for stock, and the soup they make with it can only be superb. But, when it comes to minimum effort, the trick is to produce results in a fraction of the time by combining fresh ingredients with short-cut products on the supermarket shelves.

Spinach Consommé is a life-saver for cooks in a hurry. Good served hot, but extra special chilled to a jelly in small glass bowls.

Purée until smooth in blender or processor
   300g frozen chopped spinach, with
   1-2 cups from 2 430g cans beef consommé
Transfer to saucepan with remaining consommé and boil very gently 3 minutes with
   3-4 tablespoons dry sherry
   salt and pepper to taste
Serve hot or cold, garnished with
   sour cream and a little grated nutmeg.

Lettuce Soup.

Removing only damaged outer leaves, if any, wash, shake loosely and chop roughly
   1 large lettuce
Set aside. Sauté in large saucepan
   1 large onion, chopped
   1 large carrot, chopped
   1 small capsicum, seeded and chopped, in
   2½ tablespoons butter or margarine
When onions are soft and golden, add lettuce and spoon it through other ingredients. Cover and simmer on low heat 10 minutes, stirring occasionally. Purée briefly in blender or processor (processor is best for texture and colour contrast).
Return to saucepan with
   3 large beef stock cubes, dissolved in
   5 cups hot water
Simmer 3-4 minutes to combine flavours. Stir in
   1 cup from 300g carton sour cream
   ½ cup freshly chopped parsley
Reheat without boiling. Top each serving with
   small spoonful of remaining sour cream.

OLD PERTH BOYS' SCHOOL, St. George's Terrace
now a National Trust office and display centre, comes as
a delightful surprise in a street dominated by the modern
monoliths that tower above it. It was built of sandstone
ferried up the Swan from Rocky Bay by convicts; designed by Colonial Secretary William Sanford, whose
hobby was ecclesiastical architecture; and opened as the
school's first permanent home in 1854. In those days, the
boys' education cost 2d. a week. There was no organised
sport, but they got plenty of exercise running round the
pond at the back of the school, fishing in it for gilgies
(yabbies), bird-nesting in the hills, and catching crabs
along the beaches.

Cooking instructions can confuse. *A pinch*, which must vary with finger sizes, usually means ⅛ teaspoon.

Asparagus and Artichoke Soup Surprise. Another gourmet winner when time is short — but it's a good idea to hide the cans!

A. Purée until smooth in blender
    430g can asparagus cuts
    400g can artichoke hearts, sliced
    3 cups water and liquid from cans
    3 large chicken stock cubes
Pour into large saucepan. Add
    3 tablespoons dried onion flakes
    3 tablespoons chopped parsley
    1 tablespoon brandy
    ⅛ teaspoon white pepper
Bring to boil, stirring. Cover and simmer gently 6-7 minutes. Set aside, or refrigerate. To prepare for serving: cut circles slightly larger than the rims of 6-8 1-1¼-cup ovenproof soup bowls or ramekins, from
    frozen ready rolled puff pastry
Pour a few spoons hot or reheated soup into
    2 egg yolks, beaten, and combined with
    ½ cup cream
Stir. Add to soup. Reheat, stirring — don't boil. *Almost* fill bowls. Cover with pastry (no slits), pressing it firmly around sides of bowls. Brush very lightly with
    beaten egg yolk or milk
Cook in 230C oven until puffy and golden.
*Very hot, so allow extra time for eating.

Quick Fish Soup with Flair. Nobody ever guesses it came out of a packet.

Cook, a short while ahead if you wish
    2 packets imported Lobster Soup mix, or imported Fish Soup mix, as directions
When ready to serve, pour hot or reheated soup (with egg and wine added to Fish Soup) into shallow flameproof dish. Cover lightly, so they don't sink, with
    very thin slices from peeled cucumber
Top with
    1 cup fresh breadcrumbs
Sprinkle with
    3 tablespoons grated Parmesan cheese
Grill until topping is hot and golden.

"For preventing hysterics: Carraway seeds, finely pounded, with a small proportion of ginger and salt. Spread upon bread and butter and eaten every day."
THE HOUSEWIFE'S RECEIPT BOOK, 1837.

Fish Chowder, named for the French *chaudière* — the pot in which it was traditionally cooked, is the only one in this group of soups to use all fresh ingredients. But it is still simply made, without stock.

Brown on medium heat in large saucepan
    150g smoked salt pork, diced
Stir in
    1 medium onion, finely chopped
Cook until soft. Stir in
    2 cups water
    3 cups small cubes of peeled potatoes
Bring to boil. Reduce heat and simmer until potatoes are just cooked. Stir in
    900g W.A. dhufish (or cod) fillets, well boned and skinned and cut into small squares
Boil gently 5 minutes or until fish is cooked. Stir in gently
    1 cup fresh breadcrumbs
    4 cups milk and 1 cup cream
    ⅛ teaspoon white pepper
Heat very gently without boiling. Swirl in
    2 tablespoons butter or margarine
Serve piping hot, garnished with
    finely chopped parsley.

Almond Soup.

In large saucepan sauté carefully until golden, stirring so they do not burn
    225g slivered almonds, in
    2-2½ tablespoons butter or margarine
Transfer to blender or processor, saving a few for garnish. Put aside. Cook in same pan
    1 medium potato, peeled and sliced, in
    1¼ cups water
Cook until potato is soft. Add potato and liquid to almonds with
    1 teaspoon each mustard and paprika
    2 teaspoons sugar
    1½ tablespoons flour
Blend 20 seconds or so. Return to pan with
    2 large chicken stock cubes, dissolved in
    4 cups hot water
Stir to blend. Simmer, covered, 15 minutes.
Set aside until required. Reheat. Stir in
    1 300ml carton cream
    1 tablespoon sherry and salt to taste
Reheat, stirring, without letting soup boil.
Serve garnished with reserved almonds.

Entrées

Curried Fruit Cocktail. An original and delectable start to a meal.

A. Drain and combine in flameproof dish
    1 425g can apricot halves
    1 425g can pear halves, sliced
    1 425g can sliced cling peaches
    1 425g can pitted black cherries
    1 440g can unsweetened pineapple pieces
Add and mix in
    90g pitted prunes
    ½ cup brown sugar
    4 tablespoons unsalted butter
    1¼ teaspoons curry powder
Cook, uncovered, in 180C oven 1 hour. Serve warm. If cooked ahead, refrigerate and reheat gently on stove.
*Try it, as well, as an equally original sauce with a cold buffet.

Cheese Puffs look and taste like soufflés — very impressive — but are no trouble to make.

Divide evenly between 6 1½-cup or 8 1-cup well greased soufflé pots or ramekins
    180g tasty Cheddar cheese, grated
Pat down lightly. Stand pots on baking sheet.
Beat together briefly in bowl
    8 eggs
    ⅔ cup cream
    4 tablespoons flour
    1 teaspoon mustard powder
    ¾ teaspoon salt
    ¼ teaspoon white pepper
Pour equal quantity into each pot (it's easiest from a jug) and bake in 170C oven 30 minutes or until puffed up and golden.
*Have everyone waiting and serve immediately, before they have time to fall.

Leftover juice from canned fruit can be combined and frozen until required as a jelly or sauce. For sauce, heat with a little cornflour dissolved in equal amount sherry or water; stir until thickened and smooth.

Cheese and Mushroom Pudding — 'Pudding' as in Steak and Kidney. A warm and filling entrée, ideal for winter.

A. Combine over medium heat
   3 tablespoons butter or margarine, melted
   3 tablespoons flour
Remove from heat and add
   2 cups milk
Cook, stirring, until sauce thickens. Add
   200g Swiss cheese, grated
Off heat, stir until cheese melts. Beat in
   4 eggs, one by one
Put aside. For filling, sauté lightly
   90g mushrooms, chopped, with
   2 tablespoons chopped shallots, in
   1 tablespoon oil and
   1 tablespoon butter or margarine
Sprinkle into pan and stir in well
   1 tablespoon flour, followed by
   4 tablespoons cream
   ½ teaspoon salt and ¼ teaspoon pepper
Stir over medium heat until thickened.
To assemble, put half cheese mixture in large soufflé or similar dish, or 6-8 ramekins. Add filling. Top with remaining mixture. Cook uncovered (or refrigerate, covered, until required, then cook) in 180C oven 1 hour for large dish, 40 minutes for small ones, or until a knife comes out clean.

Herring Hors D'Oeuvre. Not a recipe, but a handy idea when you want a light start to a meal and have no time to cook it.

Allowing 2 jars for 6 people, 3 jars for 8, drain in colander
   2-3 170g jars herring and onion in brine
Cut into approx. 2½cm pieces. Arrange on gratin or other attractive flat dish.
Cover with tiny thin slices from
   1 peeled eating apple
Pour over them
   3 tablespoons cream per jar
Serve. Or, better still, chill for a couple of hours. Garnish, if you wish, with
   tiny pickled onions or sliced gherkin.

The
Main
Course

*"The post-man on his way down to Fremantle yesterday,
happened to fall in with one of the sheep which had
strayed from the flock lately driven up to a farm on the
Swan, and from the exhausted state in which he found it,
he carried it to the bush inn, a distance of about a mile
and a half, for which exertion he received 2s!!"*
                    THE PERTH GAZETTE, April 1833.

Fish

Western Australia is famous Australia-wide and over-seas for its crayfish/rock lobsters. I find their delicate flavour at its best when served cold with homemade mayonnaise or grilled, with a butter sauce, but the following recipe makes an impressive party dish. It has been streamlined for speed; for ease, it can be prepared early in the day and baked before serving.

Lobster Thermidor.

The size depends on the menu but, allowing one half per person, remove meat and coral carefully — without breaking shells — from
  3-4 lobsters, no smaller than 450g, halved
Discard sand sacks, intestinal tubes and any surplus bits and pieces. Stand shells in baking tin/s and brush lightly with
  French mustard
Slice lobster meat and sauté, stirring, 3-4 minutes in
  ¾-1 cup heated butter or margarine
Spoon into shells. Stir into unwashed pan
  1¼ cups milk
  300ml carton cream
  ¼ cup brandy
  lobster coral, finely chopped or sieved
  salt and pepper to taste
Heat, then stir in to thicken
  3 tablespoons cornflour, dissolved in
  3 tablespoons cold milk
Bring to boil. Simmer, stirring, 2-3 minutes until thick and smooth. Spoon over lobster.
Sprinkle each half shell with
  1 tablespoon grated Parmesan cheese
Dot with
  3-4 tiny knobs butter or margarine
Refrigerate. When required, bake in 200C oven 20-25 minutes or until hot and golden.
Serve each shell on a wide flat base of
  mashed potato or boiled rice, sprinkled with
  freshly chopped chives or parsley.

In Scandinavia, the average crayfish measures 7-12cm, and the average intake at the happiest parties is 20 per guest, with a swig of *akvavit* between each one!

Parsley washed in hot water has a better flavour and chops more easily.

Party Crab on a Budget. 340g for 6-8 people!

A. Have ready
    225g bow or corkscrew-shaped pasta, cooked as packet directions, and drained
    400g can artichoke hearts, sliced
    340g cooked or canned crab meat, shredded
For sauce, blend on medium heat
    3 tablespoons flour, in
    3 tablespoons melted butter or margarine
Remove from heat and stir in gradually
    1¼ cups milk and 1 cup water
    1 teaspoon mustard powder
    1 large chicken stock cube, crumbled
Cook, stirring, until smooth and thickened. Remove from heat and stir in until melted
    125g from 175g grated Cheddar cheese
Cover base of large ovenproof dish with
    a thin layer of cheese sauce
Top with layers in following order
    pasta ... artichoke slices ... crab meat ... sauce
Sprinkle over top layer of sauce
    remaining 50g grated Cheddar cheese
Bake uncovered (or cover, refrigerate until required, then bake) in 180C oven 30-40 minutes or until hot and bubbly.
Brown briefly under griller if you wish.

Khat Mithi Machchi, a Parsee fish curry.

A. Have ready, cut into 2½cm squares
    1-1¼kg well boned and skinned snapper (or gemfish) fillets
Brown in heavy 2 litre casserole
    2 large onions, finely chopped, in
    3 tablespoons vegetable oil
Add to onions and fry together 2 minutes
    8 cloves garlic, crushed
    1 teaspoon mild red chilli powder
    1 teaspoon cumin seeds
    1 teaspoon ground turmeric
    ½ teaspoon salt
    3 tablespoons rolled oats
    2 tablespoons brown sugar
Add gemfish squares and mix well. Add
    1½-1¾ cups hot water
Simmer, covered, in 170C oven 40-45 minutes or until cooked. Serve very hot (or refrigerate, reheat and serve) with
    chopped red capsicum garnish
    boiled rice.

A Splendid Fish Casserole.

Allowing 1 piece per person, lay in greased casserole half quantity of
  6-8 fillets W.A. dhufish (barramundi or cod), approx. 170g each, well boned and skinned
Top with half quantity of
  425g can tomatoes, drained and chopped
Sauté until soft
  2 medium-large onions, very finely sliced and separated into rings, in
  2½ tablespoons unsalted butter or margarine
Top fish and tomatoes with half quantity of onions. Repeat layers, and seal tightly with aluminium foil and lid. Bake in 180C oven 30-45 minutes or until fish is cooked.
Transfer at least 1 cup fish juices to small saucepan, tipping dish carefully, or with spoon or bulb baster.
Stir in and heat gently without boiling
  3 tablespoons cream
  1½ tablespoons brandy
  salt and pepper to taste
Pour over fish and serve. Or keep, covered, in very low oven up to 30 minutes.

Zarzuela de Mariscos, Spanish seafood stew.

A. In 5-6 litre flameproof casserole, sauté until onions are translucent and soft
  2 medium onions, finely chopped
  1 medium red and green capsicum, seeded and finely chopped
  2 cloves garlic, finely chopped, in
  ¼ cup Spanish or other olive oil
Remove from heat and add
  900g large green prawns, shelled, deveined and cut into small bite-size pieces
  800g W.A. dhufish (cod) or similar fillets, well boned and skinned, cut into 2½cm pieces
  1 810g can tomatoes, chopped, with juice
  ½ 200g can Spanish sweet red pimentos, drained and chopped
  ½ cup slivered almonds
  ½ cup dry white wine and ⅓ cup brandy
  1 teaspoon salt and ⅛ teaspoon pepper
Cook in 200C oven 1 hour. If cooked ahead, refrigerate and reheat.
Simmer 10 minutes before serving with
  1 500g jar shelled oysters, drained
Serve in bowls with
  finely chopped parsley garnish
  crusty bread, to mop up the sauce.

FREMANTLE MUSEUM AND ARTS CENTRE,
is a magnificent example of present-day attitudes to
"purposeful preservation". Built by convict labour, overlooking the sea and using local limestone, jarrah and
she-oak, it was opened as a Lunatic Asylum for male
and female convicts in 1885 but (as if they had not trou-
bles enough) was condemned 15 years later after a
government enquiry into their treatment.

It was then used as an old women's home, a training hospital for midwives, and a barracks for US servicemen in World War II, but became derelict and vandalised and earmarked for demolition. Now scrupulously restored, with the co-operation of the City of Fremantle and the State Government of Western Australia, it does full justice to its reputation as one of the most distinguished groups of buildings in Australia.

Poultry

Turkey in a Pot. Think of Christmas, think of roast turkey. But I have never understood why; it can be so dry and dreary cooked this way. Braising it instead makes all the difference — at any time of year.

A. Allow to thaw completely
    1 frozen turkey, minimum 3kg
If using giblets and neck for stock instead of cubes, cover with water and boil gently while preparing turkey. Cut it into serving pieces and brown in batches in large frypan, in
    125g butter or margarine and
    1 tablespoon oil
Transfer to 5-6 litre flameproof casserole.
In frypan, cook, stirring, until soft
    200g rindless bacon, chopped
Add to turkey with slotted spoon. Sauté in remaining fat
    2 large onions, finely chopped
    325g celery, finely chopped
When soft, spoon onto turkey. Drain fat from pan and stir in
    2 cups strained giblet, or beef cube, stock
Pour into pot with scrapings and add
    2 large peeled potatoes, diced
    3 medium peeled granny smith apples, diced
    150g seeded raisins, roughly chopped
    5 juniper berries, crushed
    1 bay leaf, crumbled
    1 teaspoon salt and ½ teaspoon pepper
Cover pot tightly and cook in 180C oven 2 hours or until tender. Juices can be left as is. To thicken, add
    2 tablespoons cornflour, dissolved in equal quantity of water
Stir in and simmer 2-3 minutes on stove.
Serve. Or refrigerate and reheat.

The penalty for stealing 3d worth of flour in Australia in the 1850s was 200 strokes with the lash.

OLD COURT HOUSE, Supreme Court Gardens, Perth was erected in 1836-37, close to the original river foreshore, and has served a multitude of purposes from church to theatre; it now houses the Law Society. One of the city's oldest surviving buildings, it began life with white calico instead of glass in the windows.

Duckling Braised with Red Cabbage.

A. Allow to thaw
   2 frozen ducklings, minimum 1¾kg each
When thawed, wash and dry with paper towelling. Cut into serving pieces and place, skin side up, in greased baking dish or dishes.
Roast, uncovered, in 200C oven 1 hour, until browned, basting occasionally.
While ducks cook, shred finely
   1 medium red cabbage, approx. 1½kg
Cover with boiling water to blanch 5 minutes.
Drain. In large bowl, top with
   ½ cup lemon juice, to preserve colour
In heavy flameproof 5-6 litre casserole, brown
   200g smoked salt pork, diced very small
Stir in with pork and cook until soft
   2 medium onions, finely chopped
Add and mix together
   red cabbage and lemon juice
   2 cups dry red wine
   6 juniper berries, crushed
   2 bay leaves, crumbled
   1 tablespoon sugar and ¼ teaspoon pepper
Cover. Cook gently on stove or in 150C oven 30 minutes. Stir in
   3 tablespoons cornflour, dissolved in
   ½ cup cold water with ½ teaspoon salt
Mix duck pieces through cabbage. Cover and cook in 180C oven 1½ hours. Serve, or refrigerate and reheat when required.

Dill seeds were called *Meeting House seeds* by early American settlers, who chewed them at prayer meetings to relieve the monotony of boring sermons.

Lemon Chicken, Mushrooms and Capers mix and match beautifully.

A. Brown quickly in batches in deep frying-pan, allowing 2 pieces per person
  6-8 each chicken thighs and legs, in
    100-125g butter or margarine
Transfer with slotted spoon to casserole.
Drain any fat from pan, and stir in off heat
  ½ cup lemon juice
  4 tablespoons French capers, drained
  1½ teaspoons salt and 1 teaspoon paprika
Over medium heat, stir in gradually — they reduce as they cook
  450g flat mushrooms, sliced
Bring to boil, stirring, and pour over chicken. Cover tightly. Cook in 170C oven 45-60 minutes or until tender.
Serve (or refrigerate, reheat and serve) with sauce spooned up and over chicken.

African Chicken with Peanut Sauce. Even the fussiest eaters enjoy it.

A. Cut into serving pieces
  2 small chickens, approx. 1¼kg each
Sauté until golden in batches, in
  3 tablespoons butter or margarine
Transfer to flameproof casserole.
Sauté in same pan until soft and golden
  1 medium onion, sliced
Spoon onto chicken.
In large bowl or jug, dissolve
  1 large chicken cube
  2 teaspoons curry powder, in
  2½ cups boiling water
Stir in until blended and smooth
  235g jar crunchy peanut butter
Pour over chicken and bring to boil. Cover and simmer on stove, or in 150C oven, 30-40 minutes or until tender.
Serve, or refrigerate and reheat when required.
Garnish with
  salted peanuts.

"To beat eggs quickly without a whisk, use three forks instead of one ... the eggs will be beaten in a quarter the time."
THE AUSTRALIAN HOUSEHOLD GUIDE, Perth 1916.

PERTH TOWN HALL, Hay and Barrack Streets
was built by convict labour in the style of the old European market hall, with strong Tudor influence, and was opened on June 1, 1870, by Governor Weld who also announced that W.A. had been granted representative government. Bishop Hale prayed that "no rash words be spoken here to stir up strife and angry passions."

FREMANTLE TOWN HALL, King's Square
was opened on June 22, 1887 and cost £15,000 — about
ten years of Council revenue! The opening was not un-
eventful. The licensee of a local hotel shot and killed the
Councillor who wouldn't let him in to attend a ball cele-
brating Queen Victoria's golden jubilee, because he was
drunk, and was duly hanged for it.

Meat

Beef Stroganoff, a Russian dish named for the general said to have invented it.

A. Get your friendly butcher to remove all fat and sinew, cut into 1¼cm-thick slices against the grain, and pound flat
 scotch fillet or fillet steak, approx. 1¼-1⅓kg when trimmed
Cut into thin strips, about 5 cm long. Reserve.
In heavy, deep frying-pan, sauté, stirring, until they start to brown
 3 medium onions, finely chopped, in
 1½ tablespoons butter or margarine
Transfer to large flameproof casserole.
In frying-pan, brown a layer of steak pieces at a time over high heat, stirring, in
 3 tablespoons butter or margarine
Add to onions, with scrapings. Sauté in frying pan 4-5 minutes, stirring again
 450g mushrooms, thinly sliced, in
 1 tablespoon butter or margarine
Add to meat. Simmer in frypan 2-3 minutes
 ½ cup dry white wine
Stir in until blended
 1½ cartons sour cream
 1 teaspoon lemon juice
 1 teaspoon prepared English mustard
 salt and pepper to taste
Pour into casserole. Mix well. Cook in 180C oven 30-40 minutes, and serve. Or refrigerate and reheat gently when required.

Pork in Foil. People who normally don't eat pork because it is too rich for them, enjoy this without even realising it *is* pork.

Combine and leave 5 minutes or so to thicken
 1 packet French onion soup
 scant ¼ cup cold water
Lay on heavy duty aluminium foil, large enough to completely enclose it
 1¼kg-1½kg piece lean pork neck
Spread soup paste on both sides and wrap in foil thoroughly, so juices don't escape. Cook in baking tin in 170C oven 70 minutes per kg or until tender. Carve in foil, opened at table. Or on hot dish, with juices in jug.
*If you never eat pork, cook a piece of blade steak the same way, for 1 hour per kg.

31

PROCLAMATION TREE, Fremantle
Still growing and spreading, this Moreton Bay fig tree
was planted to commemorate Western Australia's Procla-
mation Day on October 21, 1890, which celebrated the
granting of responsible government and a new constitu-
tion to 'the Colony': it became a State after federation in
1901.

Veal Paupiettes, French cousins of the English beef olive, were cooked for the first time in 1735.

A. Allowing 1½ per person, spread out
   9-12 large veal escalopes, approx. 90g each, beaten
     thin and flat
For stuffing, mix together thoroughly
   100g from 150g fresh breadcrumbs
   2 tablespoons lemon juice
   2 tablespoons finely chopped chives
   1 teaspoon finely chopped basil*
   1 teaspoon finely chopped marjoram*
    (*half quantities if dried)
   ½ teaspoon salt and ¼ teaspoon pepper
Cover escalopes with thin layer of stuffing. Top each one with
   thin slice of prosciutto, koppa or ham, cut to size.
Roll up tightly. Tie with dental floss (better than string) and brown all over in large flameproof casserole, on gentle heat, in
   120g butter or margarine and
   1 tablespoon oil
Remove from pan. Sauté in remaining fat until lightly browned
   3 large onions, sliced
Place paupiettes on onions. Pour over them
   2 cups dry white wine,
    or 1 cup wine and 1 cup beef cube stock
Bring to boil. Cover. Simmer gently on stove or in 150C oven 1 hour or until tender. If cooked ahead, refrigerate and reheat gently when required.
Remove paupiettes. Cover to keep warm. Thicken sauce with
   remaining 50g breadcrumbs
Simmer, stirring, 2-3 minutes. Return the paupiettes and spoon sauce over them.
Garnish with
   chopped chives

Kuzu Kapama, Turkish lamb and vegetables.

A. First: wipe, slice and drain in colander
    2 medium aubergines (eggplants)
      generously sprinkled with salt
Brown on high heat in batches in heavy pan
    1¼kg lean lamb, roughly cubed by butcher, in
    3½ tablespoons olive oil
Transfer with slotted spoon to 5-6 litre casserole. Sprinkle with
    1 teaspoon each sugar and garlic salt
Add, in following order
    4 medium unpeeled tomatoes, sliced
    2 large leeks, trimmed, halved lengthwise, rinsed well,
      and sliced
    2 medium capsicums, seeded and sliced
    3 medium unpeeled zucchini, sliced
    aubergine slices, well rinsed and dried
    3 large potatoes, peeled and sliced,
      or 2 240g cans, rinsed and sliced
Combine in basin
    240g can tomato paste
    equal quantity of water
    1 teaspoon dried oregano (double if fresh)
    1 teaspoon salt and ¼ teaspoon pepper
Mix well and pour over potatoes. Cover. Bake in 180C oven 1¼-1½ hours or until cooked.
Serve. Or refrigerate and reheat when required.

Bundanoon Pork with Vermouth and Cream.
Especially good, and not over-rich.

Allowing 1 per person, trim rind and fat from
    6-8 large 2cm-thick loin pork chops
Set aside. In heavy pan, brown very lightly
    3 large onions, chopped
    4 cloves garlic, chopped
    4 medium peeled apples, sliced small, in
    ⅓ cup olive oil
Spoon into 5-6 litre casserole. In frying-pan, lightly brown chops on both sides. Place on top of onion and apple. Sprinkle with
    2 teaspoons fresh rosemary, finely chopped,
      or 1 teaspoon dried
Stir into frypan
    1½ cups dry vermouth
Heat and pour on chops, with scrapings. Add
    ¾ teaspoon salt and ¼ teaspoon pepper
    1½ cups cream
Cover and cook in 180C oven 1½ hours or until chops are tender. Garnish with
    chopped rosemary or parsley

36 DEVON ROAD, Swanbourne
*was built on land opened up by the Perth-to-Fremantle
Railway in 1880. It was part of the first subdivision of
ten-acre lots given as good behaviour bonuses to pen-
sioner soldiers who had fought bravely in the Crimean
and Maori Wars.*
*A picture-book house, lovingly restored before it was
fashionable to do so, it is filled with Victorian memora-
bilia, still has walls of the original pressed tin.*

Spicy Meatballs. An econòmical party dish.

A. For about 48 meatballs, combine thoroughly
   1kg good quality minced beef
   80g soft white breadcrumbs
   2 eggs, lightly beaten with a fork
   1 medium onion, finely chopped
   1 teaspoon salt and ½ teaspoon pepper
Shape into 2½cm balls. In frying-pan, brown in
   ¼ cup oil, adding more if necessary
Transfer each batch with slotted spoon to large casserole. Drain off any fat. Stir in
   ½ cup water
Pour into a basin with scrapings. Stir in
   ¼ cup soy sauce
   1 cup beef cube stock
   6 juniper berries, crushed
   4 cloves garlic, crushed
   25g fresh ginger, finely chopped
   2 tablespoons cornflour, dissolved in equal quantity
     of water
Mix well and pour over meatballs. Cover and cook in 200C oven 30-40 minutes.
Serve, or refrigerate and reheat.

Gypsy Pie. Simple, beautifully flavoured, with no 'rabbit taste'. It's interesting that it contains no onions and doesn't need any.

Cut into 5cm pieces and soak overnight
   1 rabbit, 900g dressed weight, in water to cover, with
   1 tablespoon salt
Next day, drain rabbit and pat dry with paper towelling. Put into large plastic bag. Remove fat and sinew and cut into 2½cm cubes
   500g blade or similar stewing steak
Add to plastic bag, and toss with rabbit, in
   3 tablespoons flour
Put into 2 litre pie dish. Add
   200g rindless bacon, cut into small pieces
   2 small beef cubes, dissolved in
   1 cup hot water
   2 tablespoons freshly chopped parsley
   ⅛ teaspoon dried thyme and ¼ teaspoon pepper
Stir well to mix. Cover, as instructions, with
   frozen ready rolled short crust pastry
Make slit in centre and glaze with
   milk or beaten egg yolk
Cover and cook in 180C oven 3 hours, taking care pastry does not burn. If it looks as if it might be going to, cover with foil.

Veal Chops with Crab Sauce. Very good, but must be cooked a day ahead so veal becomes tender and absorbs the sauce.

Allowing 1 per person, brown in heavy frypan
    6-8 veal chops, approx. 225g each, in
    5 tablespoons butter or margarine and
    3 tablespoons vegetable oil
Transfer to well greased 5-6 litre casserole.
Pour fat into a saucepan. Stir in
    4 tablespoons flour
Heat, stirring, until bubbly. Off heat, add
    1 cup each milk and cream
Stir over heat until thickened. Add off heat
    1 cup water
    170-185g cooked or canned crab meat, well
      shredded
    2 tablespoons lemon juice
    1 tablespoon madeira or sherry
    10 drops tabasco sauce
    ½ teaspoon chopped thyme (¼ teaspoon dried)
    ½ teaspoon salt and ¼ teaspoon pepper
Mix well. Pour over chops. Cover. Cook 1¼ hours in 170C oven. Refrigerate. Heat next day, covered, in 170C oven ½-¾ hour.

Braised Beef Short Ribs. Described by the friend who gave me the recipe as not exactly elegant, but gutsy and good.

A. Allowing 2 per person, brown on all sides in batches in heavy frying-pan
    12-16 beef short ribs, in
    150ml oil
Put into 5-6 litre casserole.
Sauté in remaining oil until soft
    3 large onions, chopped
Add to meat. Drain off any oil and stir in
    3 large beef stock cubes, dissolved in
    3 cups hot water
Add stock and scrapings to meat, with
    375g carrots, sliced in rounds
    4 tablespoons tomato paste
    2 bay leaves and 3 cloves garlic, crushed
    2 teaspoons dried oregano (double if fresh)
    2 teaspoons salt and 1 teaspoon pepper
Stir to mix. Cover. Cook 2½-3 hours in 180C oven, until meat is falling off bones.
Serve, or refrigerate and reheat when required.

FREMANTLE MARKETS
Notable for their design, which won a competition in
1897, with the original iron gates and the reproduced
bull-nosed verandah awnings. A centre of colourful activ-
ity on Fridays and Saturdays, they were refurbished and
reopened to the public in 1975.

Pilafi, an eastern rice dish spelt and cooked dif-
ferently from one country to another. This version, with
lamb, comes from Greece.

Brown lightly in batches in heavy frying-pan
    750g lamb from leg, cut into small cubes by butcher
    6-8 lamb kidneys, trimmed and cubed, in
    3 tablespoons butter or margarine
Set aside. In 5-6 litre flameproof casserole, sauté until
soft and golden
    2 medium onions, chopped
    2 cloves garlic, chopped, in
    3 tablespoons butter or margarine
Stir in and cook 3 minutes, adding fat if necessary
    2½ cups long grain rice
Stir in lamb and kidney cubes, with
    3 large chicken stock cubes, dissolved in
    5 cups boiling water
    1 cup slivered almonds and/or pine nuts
    1 cup sultanas
    1 red capsicum, seeded and thinly sliced
    3 tablespoons chopped parsley
    ½ teaspoon salt and ¼ teaspoon pepper
Bring to boil, stirring. Cover. Simmer gently on stove or
in 170C oven, without stirring, 30 minutes or until liq-
uid is absorbed and rice just cooked . . . casserole can be
kept hot in a pan of lightly simmering water.
Fluff with fork and serve with
    a large bowl of natural yoghurt.

Lamb Chops Baked with Mushrooms in aluminium foil packages means you don't have to leave your guests while you grill them.

Allowing 1 each, trim and brown on high heat
   6-8 large thick loin lamb chops, in
   1½ tablespoons oil
Drain on paper towelling. Place each chop in centre of approx. 30cm-square sheet heavy duty aluminium foil. Top each one with
   5-6 small button mushrooms, halved
   2 tablespoons chopped shallots
   a light sprinkle finely chopped mint
   a generous sprinkle salt and pepper
   2 tablespoons natural yoghurt or sour cream
Enclose completely with foil, so juices cannot escape. Cook on baking sheet in 180C oven 20-30 minutes, just until chops are cooked.
Serve in foil with jacket potatoes and a salad.

Sauerbraten, a popular Central European sweet-and-sour pot roast.

A. Place in china or glass container
   1½-1¾kg piece round or similar steak
For marinade, heat together but do not boil
   2 cups each wine vinegar and water
   2 each large onions and carrots, sliced
   10 peppercorns and 2 bay leaves
   ¼ cup sugar and ¼ teaspoon ground thyme
Pour over steak. Cover. Refrigerate 2-3 days, turning meat twice a day. Then remove it and dry with paper towelling, saving marinade. Dust meat lightly with flour. Brown all over in large heavy flameproof casserole, in
   2-3 tablespoons very hot oil
Add unstrained marinade and cover. Cook in 150C oven 2½ hours or until meat pierces easily with tip of sharp knife.
If cooked ahead, strain marinade, return to meat in casserole, and refrigerate.
Put hot or reheated meat on heated platter.
For sauce, heat strained marinade, stirring until smooth and thickened, with
   ¼ cup brown sugar
   100g imported honeycake crumbs,
      or 10 ginger nut biscuits, broken up
Serve meat sliced, topped with sauce, with boiled potatoes and boiled red cabbage.

Vegetables and Side Dishes

Zucchini de Luxe looks and tastes superb. It can be served as a side dish, a light main dish, or as an entrée.

Wash and grate, unpeeled, into colander
   6 large zucchini, approx. 1¼kg
Sprinkle with
   1 teaspoon salt
Let drain ½ hour. Then combine in bowl with
   75g mild Cheddar cheese, grated
   75g tasty Cheddar cheese, grated
   6 large eggs, well beaten with
   ½ teaspoon salt and ⅛ teaspoon pepper
Mix well and pour into well greased 2 litre shallow ovenproof serving dish. Bake in 220C oven 40 minutes or until hot and golden.
*If there is liquid in dish after serving, it does not mean zucchini are undercooked ... it is quite a common problem with them.

Grilled Green Tomatoes, for a new look.

Allowing 1 per person, slice thickly
   6-8 green tomatoes, approx. 100g each
Sprinkle lightly with
   salt and pepper
Dip into mixture of
   1 cup fresh breadcrumbs, with
   1 teaspoon mixed chopped sage and basil,
     or ½ teaspoon dried
   2 tablespoons finely chopped chives
Place in greased shallow flameproof dish.
Dot with
   butter or margarine
Grill 10cm from medium heat 5-6 minutes each side or until lightly browned and very hot.

Troublefree Rice, cooked in the oven.

Combine in casserole
   1½ cups long grain rice
   1½ teaspoons salt
   2 tablespoons butter or margarine
Pour in
   3 cups boiling water
Stir. Cover. Bake in 180C oven 40 minutes or until rice is cooked and water absorbed. Fluff with fork before serving.

GOVERNMENT HOUSE, St. George's Terrace
With the Deanery, one of only two original residences remaining in The Terrace. Designed by Colonel E. Hender-
son of the Royal Engineers. It has been the home of all
West Australian Governors since 1864 and is noteworthy
for its elegant Flemish bondwork, the lovely variation of
colours in its bricks from wood-fired kilns, and the Tudor influence which makes it reminiscent of the Tower of
London.

Balls were held by Governor and Lady Stirling when
Government House was only a tent. They usually lasted
until daylight, because settlers crossing the river to go
home in the dark easily strayed off the ford into deep
water and quicksands. If you were fitted out like Mrs.
James Drummond, wife of the Colonial Botanist — net
frock looped up with pearl ornaments, white silk stock-
ings, blue kid gloves and ankle trousers with frills — this
was not a happy thing to happen.

Sweet and Spicy African Salad. Unusual and very nice — a sharp, fresh taste.

Boil as packet instructions
   375g brown rice
While it cooks, combine in bowl for dressing
   ½ cup oil
   4 tablespoons lemon juice
   1 tablespoon finely grated lemon rind
   1½ teaspoons salt
   ⅛ teaspoon cayenne pepper
   1 teaspoon ground coriander
   1 teaspoon ground cumin
   2 teaspoons honey
Drain rice. Rinse well. Let cool slightly, then add dressing and mix thoroughly. Add
   2 large ripe firm bananas, sliced
   1 medium cucumber, partly peeled for colour contrast, halved, seeded and sliced
   100g seeded raisins
   2 tablespoons mixed chopped nuts
Combine well. Cover and chill 2-3 hours.

Cucumber and Strawberry Salad adds a touch of glamour to cold poultry.

Arrange attractively in shallow glass dish
   2 medium cucumbers, peeled and very thinly sliced
   1 carton large firm ripe strawberries, hulled, washed, dried and sliced
Sprinkle with
   salt and pepper
   3 tablespoons tarragon vinegar,
     or white wine vinegar
Chill well before serving.

Frozen Green Beans with an added dimension.

Cook two-thirds of time specified on
   large pack frozen green beans
Drain well. Sauté in same saucepan until soft
   1 onion and 1 clove garlic, chopped, in
   3 tablespoons butter or margarine
Add beans. Cover and simmer briefly for remaining cooking time. Add
   2-3 tablespoons cream
Serve hot, garnished with
   slivered almonds or chopped herbs.

Hay and Straw makes a tasty change from potatoes. And it looks pretty.

Cook as packet instructions
   225g white flat noodles
   225g green flat noodles
Drain. Set aside. Melt in same saucepan
   3 tablespoons butter or margarine
Add noodles and
   ½ cup freshly chopped parsley
Stir over medium heat until hot. Serve with
   a bowl of grated Parmesan cheese.

Gratin Dauphinois, when you don't want a change from potatoes.

Arrange in layers in gratin or other shallow oven dish
   900g peeled potatoes, thinly sliced
   2 large onions, thinly sliced
   a sprinkle of salt and pepper
Finish with potato layer. Cover with
   150ml cream, mixed with
   3 tablespoons milk
Add more cream and milk if necessary, so liquid reaches almost to top of potatoes.
Dot with small pieces of
   butter or margarine
Cook in 180C oven 1 hour, or until potatoes are cooked and top layer is well browned.
*A gratin crust is also achieved with topping of bread-crumbs, or grated cheese.

Rice Salad can be made with leftover rice, frozen until needed. But it is more of a meal than a salad, if combined with whatever happens to be on hand at the time.

Try it with some of the following:
   raw mushrooms, thinly sliced
   tiny cubes of cheese
   olives or seedless grapes
   celery, capsicum and shallots, sliced
   julienne strips of cold meat or poultry
   cubes of seeded cucumber and melon
   anchovies, drained and chopped, etc. etc.
Then add chopped whites from
   2-3 hard-boiled eggs, reserving yolks
Moisten with equal quantities of
   salad dressing and egg mayonnaise
Season to taste. And garnish with
   finely chopped egg yolks.

WELD CLUB, *Barrack Street and Esplanade*
The Club was founded in 1871 in St George's Terrace as
a meeting place for gentlemen of substance. Later on it
moved to its present splendid quarters, the work of
Joseph Talbot Hobbs, an architect responsible for a great
many of Perth's goldrush buildings.

Sauces and Suchlike

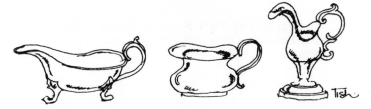

Versatile Summer Sauce to serve with hot or cold fish, with shellfish for seafood cocktail, or as a dip for chilled chicory leaves.

Combine
    ⅓ cup egg mayonnaise
    ⅓ cup sour cream or natural yoghurt
    ⅓ cup tomato ketchup
    1 teaspoon caster sugar
    2 teaspoons fresh orange juice
    salt and white pepper to taste
Cover, and chill to thicken.

Pickled Lemons go well with any cold meat. Store 3 weeks before serving.

Cut into slices or small wedges
    3 medium thin-skinned lemons
Remove seeds. Place in colander and sprinkle with
    1 tablespoon salt
Leave to drain 12 hours. Then pack into screw-top jar and cover with
    good quality olive oil
Seal and keep in cool place (not refrigerator).

Maître d'Hôtel Butter is a marvellous time-saving substitute for sauces. It is made ahead, put into serving pot or bowl, covered, and chilled until firm.

For grilled steak and fish. Mix well
    250g softened unsalted butter
    1 tablespoon lemon juice
    4 tablespoons finely chopped parsley and/or mixture
        of basil, rosemary, dill, chives
    ½ teaspoon salt and ¼ teaspoon pepper

Horseradish Butter, delicious with hot roast beef, and the sandwiches made when it's cold.

Mix well and chill as above
    250g softened unsalted butter
    3 tablespoons bottled horseradish.

To stop a pie becoming soggy, brush pastry base before filling with beaten egg white or melted butter and let stand 10 minutes.

Orange and Port Sauce is intended for roast lamb. But it also goes well with pork, ham, turkey and pheasant.

Soak in boiling water 5 minutes. Then remove peel and pith from
2 oranges
Cut into 2cm pieces. Remove seeds and purée in blender or processor with
2 tablespoons grated orange rind
2 tablespoons cranberry sauce
½ cup port
⅛ teaspoon allspice (pimento)
Simmer in small saucepan 10 minutes.
Serve hot or reheated.

Onion Sauce, adapted from an old English recipe, is equally good hot or cold with hot or cold poultry.

Boil in a little salted water until just tender
450g white onions, sliced
Drain well and purée while hot in blender or processor with
3 tablespoons butter or margarine
3 tablespoons cream
½ teaspoon salt
⅛ teaspoon white pepper
For colour contrast, serve sprinkled with
paprika.

Cheese Sauce without Flour can be stored and used as it is needed.

Melt in double boiler over boiling water
250g Cheddar cheese, chopped
When melted, stir in until smooth
¾ cup canned evaporated milk
1 teaspoon prepared English mustard
½ teaspoon salt and ⅛ teaspoon paprika
Keep in sealed jar in refrigerator. To use, put desired quantity in double boiler and thin as necessary with milk, over boiling water.

"It is a good plan when peeling onions, to put them into a bowl and to pour hot water over. This enables one to peel them very quickly and without tears."
THE AUSTRALIAN HOUSEHOLD GUIDE, Perth 1916.

After
the
Main
Course

"*Many families of respectability, we feel convinced, are deterred from emigrating in consequence of their reflecting that their children must of necessity run wild in the trackless woods of a new settlement; we rejoice, we are able to remove these scruples . . . by a reference to the establishment of a private seminary at Perth under the vigilant eye and guidance of a Gentleman of great ability, and considerable practical knowledge.*"

THE PERTH GAZETTE, March 1837.

Desserts

It is really strange about desserts. The way they intimi-
date so many people. And yet they can be unbelievably
simple.

Tortoni, for instance, named for the Italian café
proprietor who introduced ice cream made with cream
and fruit to Paris in the 18th century. An easy version,
using commercial ice cream, that gets rave reviews
every time.

Set freezer to its coldest.
Leave 1 hour out of refrigerator to soften
   2 litres best quality vanilla ice cream
Lightly brown on baking sheet in 160C oven 6-8 minutes, watching carefully so they don't burn
   ¾ cup chunky slivered almonds — not flat ones
Set aside. Combine in small bowl
   ½ cup cream
   227g jar maraschino cherries, drained and chopped
   1 cup chocolate bits,
     or dark chocolate, chopped small
   3 tablespoons brandy
   1 teaspoon each grated orange and lemon rind
In large bowl, break up softened ice cream with spoon.
Stir in cream mixture evenly. Spoon into soufflé or
serving dish. Cover with plastic wrap and freeze 2
hours.
Top with toasted almonds. Cover. Freeze at least 2
more hours.

Blender Chocolate and Orange Mousse is not
just quick and easy. It is also very light, as it is made
with milk instead of cream.

Place in blender container
   150g dark chocolate, broken up
   4 eggs
   1½ tablespoons instant coffee powder
   3 tablespoons sugar
   2 tablespoons fresh orange juice
   1 tablespoon brandy (optional)
Heat to just below boiling point
   ¾ cup milk
Add to container. Blend on high speed 2-3 minutes until smooth. Pour into 6-8 pots or small bowls. Chill to
set and serve with
   whipped cream, for anyone who wants it.

Cappuccino Cream is made in minutes.

Combine in chilled mixing bowl
    300ml carton chilled cream
    4 tablespoons caster sugar
    3 teaspoons instant coffee powder
    2½ tablespoons or miniature bottle Tia Maria
Beat briefly, just until thick. Chill in 6-8 small glasses
or pots.
Before serving, sprinkle lightly with
    drinking chocolate powder (not cocoa)

Baked Apple Sponge Pudding.

Cream together
    2 eggs
    1 cup sugar
Stir in
    ¼ cup milk
    2 tablespoons melted butter or margarine
    1 cup self-raising flour
    ¼ teaspoon powdered ginger
    ¼ teaspoon powdered cinnamon
    1 tablespoon finely grated lemon rind
    1 tablespoon lemon juice
Mix well and pour into greased 20cm cake tin or
2 litre pie dish. Spread over the top
    1 410g can unsweetened pie apple
Bake in 180C oven 1¼-1½ hours until skewer comes
out clean and pudding is golden brown.
Serve hot or warm with
    liquid cream.

Marshmallow Custard. A new twist to an
old–fashioned baked custard. Can be eaten hot but
tastes best when marshmallow topping has set in
refrigerator.

In mixing bowl, combine
    3 eggs, lightly beaten
    1 tablespoon caster sugar
    4 drops vanilla essence
Heat without boiling in small saucepan
    1 cup each milk and cream
Add to eggs, stirring all the time. Pour into soufflé or
similar dish. Top with
    20 white marshmallows
Stand in hot water in baking tin. Cook, uncovered, in
180C oven 50 minutes, or until knife inserted near
edge of custard comes out clean.

THE CLOISTERS, St. George's Terrace
Typical of Perth architecture between 1858-85, which made it unique among Australia's cities, it opened in 1858-59 as Bishop Mathew Hale's collegiate school for boys, but eventually closed for lack of pupils. The building (its eastern part added in 1863, obscuring the old schoolhouse) later served as a centre for clergy-in-training, a high school, and private housing, and was saved from 20th century demolition by public protest. The Port Macquarie fig tree in the courtyard, which also narrowly escaped extinction, is over 100 years old.

Banana Brown Betty, a variation of the traditional hot apple pudding. Not for elegant dinner parties, perhaps, but certainly perfect for an informal meal on a winter's night.

Sauté on medium heat until brown
　　4 cups small white bread cubes, without crusts, in
　　4 tablespoons butter or margarine
Slice thinly in bowl
　　6 firm ripe bananas
Spoon gently onto them
　　¾ cup brown sugar, mixed with
　　½ teaspoon cinnamon and
　　juice and grated rind of 1 lemon
Arrange bread cubes (less a few for topping), then bananas, in layers in buttered oven dish, ending with bananas. Top with
　　reserved bread cubes, crumbled
Bake 30 minutes, covered with foil, in 190C oven. Remove foil and cook further 30 minutes.
Serve hot with
　　liquid cream.

Marvellous Mocca Ice Cream.

Set freezer to its coldest.
Beat in chilled bowl until thick
　　300ml carton chilled cream
Refrigerate. Have ready
　　4 egg yolks (whites can be frozen)
Pulverise in blender
　　200g dark chocolate pieces, with
　　1½ teaspoons instant coffee powder
In small saucepan, stir
　　4 tablespoons caster sugar into
　　½ cup boiling water
Continue boiling 2 minutes. Pour immediately onto chocolate and blend briefly until smooth. Blend a few more seconds with egg yolks. Add chocolate mixture to whipped cream and beat on low speed until blended. Freeze, covered, in ice cream trays 3-4 hours or until firm. Transfer to refrigerator 20 minutes or so before serving.

It is only necessary to grease pan for the first pancake if 1 tablespoon melted butter or margarine is added to each 2 cups batter, stirred, and left to stand at least 30 minutes.

Fraises Malakoff. Not cheap, but a special occasion knockout.

Have ready
    2 cartons small ripe firm strawberries, hulled, washed, dried on paper towelling
    125g flat slivered almonds
    2 300ml cartons chilled cream, whipped thick in large chilled bowl, and refrigerated
Stir over low heat in small saucepan
    1 cup caster sugar, in
    5 tablespoons water
When dissolved, cool slightly and add
    ½ cup cointreau
    ¼ teaspoon almond essence
Stir in
    2 tablespoons gelatine, dissolved in
    ½ cup hot water
Refrigerate until it shows first signs of setting, then fold into chilled cream. In glass serving bowl, arrange in layers
    cream mixture . . . strawberries . . . almonds
Continue until ingredients are used up, finishing with strawberries and almonds. Refrigerate at least 3 hours to set.

Tipsy Apple Meringue.

Line base of 25cm china flan dish with
    sponge fingers from 150g packet
Pour over them
    ⅓ cup white rum, gin or vodka
Cover biscuits evenly with
    780g can unsweetened pie apples
Combine in small saucepan
    2 tablespoons butter or margarine
    ½ cup light brown sugar
    2 tablespoons lemon juice
    ½ teaspoon cinnamon
Stir over low heat until sugar has melted. Pour immediately over apples and spread evenly. For meringue, beat until stiff
    3 egg whites, at room temperature
Add gradually while still beating
    200g caster sugar
When smooth and shiny, cover apples completely with meringue. Swirl with fork. Bake in 180C oven 10 minutes or until lightly browned.

Cold Portuguese Walnut Pudding.

Pulverise to smooth paste
   175g canned shelled walnuts, saving a few whole
     ones for decoration
Traditionally done with mortar and pestle, but for minimum effort use blender. The secret is to add a few
nuts at a time with motor running, a hand quickly on
top so they don't escape.
Whisk together
   5 eggs
   225g sugar
   ½ teaspoon cinnamon
Add walnut paste and mix thoroughly. Put into 20cm
soufflé or similar dish. Stand in 3¾cm hot water in
baking tin. Cook, uncovered, in 180C oven about 1½
hours or until knife comes out clean. Cool, cover, and
refrigerate.
To serve, cover meringue-like top with
   whipped cream and reserved walnuts.

Cider Frappé from an old French cook book. Its
delicate flavour is hard to describe — something like
honey.

Set freezer to its coldest. Boil 2 minutes
   2 cups sweet alcoholic cider, with
   ⅔ cup caster sugar
   2½cm cinnamon stick
Allow to cool until less than lukewarm. Discard cinnamon stick and stir thoroughly into
   300ml chilled carton cream, whipped thick
Spoon into 2 ice cream trays and freeze, covered, about
5 hours until set.
Serve alone or with
   summer berry fruits.

Iced Banana Cream. Simple, attractive, delicious
and refreshing.

Set freezer to its coldest. Mash with fork
   2 large ripe (but not brown) bananas, totalling
     approx. 400g
Sprinkle with
   ½ cup caster sugar
   2 tablespoons lemon juice
Fold through
   300ml carton chilled cream, beaten thick
Freeze, covered, in 6-8 small pots or 2 ice cream trays
at least 4 hours. Serve from freezer.

Walnuts date back at least four centuries B.C. Th
Romans ate them to ensure good luck and a long life.

THE MELBOURNE HOTEL, St. George's Terrace
is a world away from the first primitive hotels of 1830,
with thatched roofs. Its florid and ornate design is typical
of the structural and social changes of the 1890s, when
the new wealth from the goldfields at Coolgardie and
Kalgoorlie transformed Perth from a "compact little
town" to a busy, bustling metropolis.

Blender Chocolate Torte, inspired by the famous Viennese Sachertorte which was created for Prince Metternich in 1832 by his chef, Franz Sacher.

Beat for a few seconds in blender
   6 eggs (instead of original 14 yolks!)
Stop beating and add in the following order
   1 teaspoon vanilla essence
   ¾ cup caster sugar
   1 cup walnut pieces
   2 tablespoons flour
   2½ teaspoons baking powder
   ⅛ teaspoon salt
   2 tablespoons cocoa
Blend at high speed 1 minute. Pour into 20cm cake tin, greased and lined with greaseproof paper. Bake in 180C oven 30 minutes or until skewer comes out clean. Remove from tin. Cool on rack.
Cover cake with layer of
   apricot conserve
For chocolate icing, melt in double saucepan over simmering water (or basin in water)
   200g cooking chocolate pieces, with
   100g butter and 2½ tablespoons vegetable oil
Stir to blend thoroughly. Cool to coating consistency. Pour on cake and smooth with metal spatula. Refrigerate until required.
Serve with
   whipped cream on the side.
*Torte can be made 1-2 days ahead, and actually improves with keeping.

WINTHROP HALL, University of Western Australia

The University, established in 1911, is said to be the greatest achievement of Dr. (later Sir) John Winthrop Hackett — dedicated Anglican, part-time owner and editor of the West Australian from 1887-1916, and trustee or committee member of every notable educational organisation in Perth — whose aim it was to see free tertiary education available to everyone with suitable academic qualifications.

GALLOP HOUSE, *Birdwood Parade, Dalkeith*
with its magnificent row of steps up to the front entrance,
overlooks the Swan River. Built by market gardener
James Gallop for one of his sons not long before his
death in 1880, it stood on 320 acres of land famous for
their grape vines. The gardens are gone now, but the
house has been completely restored as a museum.

Individual Baked Alaskas from my cousin in England. Unusual and clever, because you can make them days ahead, freeze them, and cook them when you want them.

Allow to soften at room temperature
  small carton ice cream, any flavour
Cut 6-8 2¼cm-thick slices from
  225g french sponge roll,
      or any flavour plain cake, cut to shape
Place in 1 cup soufflé pots or ramekins and saturate each slice with
  3-4 teaspoons brandy, rum or sherry
Top each one with
  2-3 tablespoons softened ice cream
For meringue topping, beat until thick
  2 egg whites, at room temperature
Add gradually, beating until stiff
  6 tablespoons caster sugar
Cover pots completely, swirling meringue into peaks with knife. Freeze uncovered. When required, put straight into 200C oven 6 minutes or until lightly browned.

Parfait au Café from my New York cousin, whose recipes are always fantastic.

Quantities are for 8, and difficult to adjust for 6; but leftovers are never a problem!
Have ready
  1½ 300ml cartons chilled cream, whipped thick in chilled bowl, and refrigerated
  1½ teaspoons instant coffee (preferably granules), dissolved in 2 teaspoons water
  6 egg yolks in large bowl
Combine over low heat in small saucepan
  150g sugar with 1½ tablespoons water
Stir occasionally until thick and syrupy, but not yet changing colour for caramel. While syrup simmers, beat egg yolks. As soon as it is ready, pour onto eggs while beating at high speed (scraping it all in as it starts to cool and set), until light and thick and almost trebled in volume.
Add coffee and blend in chilled cream. Spoon into stemmed champagne glasses or small glass bowls. Freeze uncovered at least 2 hours.
Serve garnished with a tiny sprinkle of instant coffee — and then, says my cousin, "Aaaah".

> "When dinner is finished . . . the French and other Continentals have the habit of gargling the mouth; but it is a custom no English gentlewoman should, in the slightest degree, imitate."
>
> MRS. ISABELLA BEETON, 1861.

20 QUEEN VICTORIA STREET, Fremantle
One of the very few terraces left to charm us.

Coffee

At the risk of repeating myself, but for the benefit of new readers, I have to say that this is the best time of all for me, at any dinner party. When the last of the dishes have been cleared away. When you don't need a crystal ball to tell you that the food and the wine and the guests have all worked out beautifully together. And when everyone stays sitting happily around the dining table, to enjoy the conversation and the coffee.

So the coffee has to be good! Freshly ground if possible. Certainly freshly made. And if the TV commercials have brainwashed you to believe you can only make instant, try making 'the real thing' this easy way and you'll be a convert for life.

Just heat the pot, as for tea.
Put in 1 dessertspoon fresh coffee (it's best to buy a small quantity and replace it often) for each cup.
Pour on the correct quantity of boiling water.
Stir. Cover. Let stand 3 minutes.
Then strain it into another heated pot. Or settle the grounds by sprinkling a few drops of cold water over the top.

Chocolate Truffles, served with small cups of fresh, fragrant coffee, make a perfect finish to a meal.

A day ahead, melt in basin in a saucepan of simmering water
    150g small pieces cooking chocolate
Stir in
    1 tablespoon each caster sugar and water
    100g unsalted butter
Mix well together. Remove basin. Cool and refrigerate until mixture is set but malleable. With teaspoon, take enough between the palms to shape (quickly, before it gets too soft) uneven ball approx. 2cm in diameter.
Roll in bowl of
    drinking chocolate powder
Place on plate. Repeat to make 20-24 truffles. Chill until set. Store in container in refrigerator.

Marzipan Dates have a role to play when you need an after-dinner something in a hurry. Or after a chocolate dessert, when chocolate truffles would be a bit much.
It's more of a production line exercise than a recipe. Fill large pitted dates with small rolls made from packet of soft marzipan. Insert an almond lengthwise into each one, with top rising above it.
*In France, dattes fourrés are filled with marzipan softened with a little liqueur.

Easy Metrics

A few basic conversions, for easy reference, using standard metric cups and spoons on sale here. They don't make sense mathematically, but they work.

Cup weights for solids are approximate only, as these vary considerably according to ingredients.

General:
1 teaspoon = 5 grams — 5 millilitres
1 tablespoon = 4 teaspoons = 20 grams — 20 millilitres
* BUT UK/USA tablespoon = 3 teaspoons = 15g/ml

1oz = 1½ tablespoons = 30g/ml
2oz = 3 tablespoons = ¼ cup = 60g/ml
4½oz = ½ cup = 125g/ml
8oz = ½ lb = 225g/ml
9oz = 1 cup =250g/ml
16oz = 1lb = 450g/ml = 1 USA-European pint
18oz = 500g = ½kg . . . the official equivalent of 1lb
20oz = 2½ cups = 600g/ml = 1 UK-Australian pint
   No wonder we still get confused.

Ovens:
275 Fahrenheit = 140 Celcius
300F = 150C 325F = 160C 350F = 180C 375F = 190C
400F = 200C 425F = 220C 450F = 230C

Utensils:
1 inch = 2½ centimetres
8in = 20cm 10in = 25cm 12in = 30cm 15in = 37½cm

Pink everlastings.
bloom in carpets in the
spring, and when dried
are sent all over the world.

ACKNOWLEDGMENTS
My thanks to the librarians at Perth's Battye Library of Western Australian History for the wealth of material put at my disposal. And to the people of Perth and Fremantle who helped make it come alive for me.
Readers unfamiliar with Perth will like to know that the cover features the Barracks Archway, all that is left of the building designed in 1863 to house the veteran soldiers who came from England to guard convicts transported as a labour force.

Index

After the Main Course